Senior Health, A(

Habit Tracker • Fitness Journal • Daily Affirmations • Goal Setting • Classes & Clubs List • Monthly Guided Journal • Friends Contact Book
Health Digest

Simple Start Guides
Everett, WA

Senior Health, Activity & Fitness Diary:
Habit Tracker • Fitness Journal • Daily Affirmations • Goal Setting • Classes & Clubs List • Monthly Guided Journal • Friends Contact Book • Health Digest

Created by Simple Start Guides
Everett, WA 98201

© 2019 D.A. Byrne
All rights reserved. No portion of this book may be reproduced in any form without permission, except as permitted by U.S. copyright law.

For permissions contact:
SimpleStartGuides@gmail.com

Cover and Title Page Photos copyright by Cindy L Shebley
© Cindy L Shebley
Used with Permission

Interior Photos:
Photos by Gareth Williams https://www.flickr.com/photos/gareth1953/
Page: *Staying Active, Staying Well*
Chanctonbury Ring-Mar 2013-Fellow Dog Walkers Descend from the Summit
Creative Commons License 2.0 Attribution (CC BY 2.0)
Page: *Achievements & Goals, Clubs, Classes & Hobbies*
The Horniman Museum Garden - Aug 2016 - 6 across, 7 letters
Creative Commons License 2.0 Generic (CC BY 2.0)

Page: *Personal & Medical Info & Contacts*
Photo by Rafael Montilla
https://www.flickr.com/photos/rafaelmontilla
Bayfront Park Miami-Free Yoga Classes
Creative Commons License 2.0 Attribution-Share Alike (CC BY-SA)

ISBN: 9781096690252

TABLE of CONTENTS

STAYING ACTIVE, STAYING WELL
- 12 Month Fitness and Social Habit Tracker
- Detailed Daily Fitness & Activity Journal

ACHIEVEMENTS, & GOALS, CLUBS, CLASSES & HOBBIES
- 12 Month Daily Accomplishments, Affirmations & Goals Diary
- Skills I Want to Learn List
- Clubs, Classes & Meetings List & Planner
- 12 Item Guided Prompt Journal

PERSONAL & MEDICAL INFO & CONTACTS
- Mood Tracker
- Medical Providers Contact Book
- Pharmacy n& Medication List
- 12 Month Health & Vitals Tracker
- Family & Friends Address Book

HOW TO USE THIS JOURNAL

Staying Active - Staying Well

This section includes a twelve month habit tracker that allows you to mark days for both fitness and social activities.

Write the month and year at the top of the page, then place a check in any box on a date when you performed that activity.

Use the empty columns at the top of the page to enter your own activities.

Daily Fitness & Activity Journal

Use these pages to record your walks, gym visits, yoga practice etc. in more detail. Use the lined section of the page to record thoughts, plans, progress, or problems you encounter.

Over time, the Habit Tracker and the Fitness Journal will help you build a reliable routine that will help you stay fit and active.

Although most health authorities recommend that seniors get 2.5 hours of moderate aerobic activity every week, the amount, duration, and exertion varies from one person to the next..

Whatever your current fitness level, exercise will make you feel better.

Of course, consult your doctor before beginning any new exercise routine.

Accomplishments & Goals, Clubs, Classes & Hobbies

List your daily goals and accomplishments. Use affirmations to encourage yourself whenever you need a pat on the back. When you look back over the year, you'll be amazed at how much you have achieved!

There is a Prompt journal with one page per month. Use the suggested topic (the prompt at the top of the page) to get your creative juices flowing.

You don't need to follow these prompts in order. You don't even have to stick to the suggestions if there are topics you'd rather explore instead.

The important thing is to think about what makes you happy.

Staying Active

Staying Well

DAILY ACTIVITY: FITNESS

Month _____

Year _____

Day	Walking	Swimming	Jogging	Yoga	Stretching	Bicycling	Gardening	Resistance	Dancing	Golf	Tai Chi	Pickle Ball			Enjoyable
1															☹ 😀
2															☹ 😀
3															☹ 😀
4															☹ 😀
5															☹ 😀
6															☹ 😀
7															☹ 😀
8															☹ 😀
9															☹ 😀
10															☹ 😀
11															☹ 😀
12															☹ 😀
13															☹ 😀
14															☹ 😀
15															☹ 😀
16															☹ 😀
17															☹ 😀
18															☹ 😀
19															☹ 😀
20															☹ 😀
21															☹ 😀
22															☹ 😀
23															☹ 😀
24															☹ 😀
25															☹ 😀
26															☹ 😀
27															☹ 😀
28															☹ 😀
29															☹ 😀
30															☹ 😀
31															☹ 😀

DAILY ACTIVITY: SOCIAL LIFE

Month _____

Year _____

Day	Visit Friends	Eat Out	Volunteer	Class	Play Cards	Shopping	Sr. Center	Painting	Mall Walk	Babysit	Walk Dog				Enjoyable
1															☹ 🙂
2															☹ 🙂
3															☹ 🙂
4															☹ 🙂
5															☹ 🙂
6															☹ 🙂
7															☹ 🙂
8															☹ 🙂
9															☹ 🙂
10															☹ 🙂
11															☹ 🙂
12															☹ 🙂
13															☹ 🙂
14															☹ 🙂
15															☹ 🙂
16															☹ 🙂
17															☹ 🙂
18															☹ 🙂
19															☹ 🙂
20															☹ 🙂
21															☹ 🙂
22															☹ 🙂
23															☹ 🙂
24															☹ 🙂
25															☹ 🙂
26															☹ 🙂
27															☹ 🙂
28															☹ 🙂
29															☹ 🙂
30															☹ 🙂
31															☹ 🙂

DAILY ACTIVITY: FITNESS

Month _____

Year _____

Day	Walking	Swimming	Jogging	Yoga	Stretching	Bicycling	Gardening	Resistance	Dancing	Golf	Tai Chi	Pickle Ball			Enjoyable
1															😐 😃
2															😐 😃
3															😐 😃
4															😐 😃
5															😐 😃
6															😐 😃
7															😐 😃
8															😐 😃
9															😐 😃
10															😐 😃
11															😐 😃
12															😐 😃
13															😐 😃
14															😐 😃
15															😐 😃
16															😐 😃
17															😐 😃
18															😐 😃
19															😐 😃
20															😐 😃
21															😐 😃
22															😐 😃
23															😐 😃
24															😐 😃
25															😐 😃
26															😐 😃
27															😐 😃
28															😐 😃
29															😐 😃
30															😐 😃
31															😐 😃

DAILY ACTIVITY: SOCIAL LIFE

Month _____

Year _____

Day	Visit Friends	Eat Out	Volunteer	Class	Play Cards	Shopping	Sr. Center	Painting	Mall Walk	Babysit	Walk Dog				Enjoyable
1															☹ 😃
2															☹ 😃
3															☹ 😃
4															☹ 😃
5															☹ 😃
6															☹ 😃
7															☹ 😃
8															☹ 😃
9															☹ 😃
10															☹ 😃
11															☹ 😃
12															☹ 😃
13															☹ 😃
14															☹ 😃
15															☹ 😃
16															☹ 😃
17															☹ 😃
18															☹ 😃
19															☹ 😃
20															☹ 😃
21															☹ 😃
22															☹ 😃
23															☹ 😃
24															☹ 😃
25															☹ 😃
26															☹ 😃
27															☹ 😃
28															☹ 😃
29															☹ 😃
30															☹ 😃
31															☹ 😃

DAILY ACTIVITY: FITNESS

Month _____

Year _____

Day	Walking	Swimming	Jogging	Yoga	Stretching	Bicycling	Gardening	Resistance	Dancing	Golf	Tai Chi	Pickle Ball		Enjoyable
1														☹ 😃
2														☹ 😃
3														☹ 😃
4														☹ 😃
5														☹ 😃
6														☹ 😃
7														☹ 😃
8														☹ 😃
9														☹ 😃
10														☹ 😃
11														☹ 😃
12														☹ 😃
13														☹ 😃
14														☹ 😃
15														☹ 😃
16														☹ 😃
17														☹ 😃
18														☹ 😃
19														☹ 😃
20														☹ 😃
21														☹ 😃
22														☹ 😃
23														☹ 😃
24														☹ 😃
25														☹ 😃
26														☹ 😃
27														☹ 😃
28														☹ 😃
29														☹ 😃
30														☹ 😃
31														☹ 😃

DAILY ACTIVITY: SOCIAL LIFE

Month _____

Year _____

Day	Visit Friends	Eat Out	Volunteer	Class	Play Cards	Shopping	Sr. Center	Painting	Mall Walk	Babysit	Walk Dog				Enjoyable
1															😕 🙂
2															😕 🙂
3															😕 🙂
4															😕 🙂
5															😕 🙂
6															😕 🙂
7															😕 🙂
8															😕 🙂
9															😕 🙂
10															😕 🙂
11															😕 🙂
12															😕 🙂
13															😕 🙂
14															😕 🙂
15															😕 🙂
16															😕 🙂
17															😕 🙂
18															😕 🙂
19															😕 🙂
20															😕 🙂
21															😕 🙂
22															😕 🙂
23															😕 🙂
24															😕 🙂
25															😕 🙂
26															😕 🙂
27															😕 🙂
28															😕 🙂
29															😕 🙂
30															😕 🙂
31															😕 🙂

DAILY ACTIVITY: FITNESS

Month _____

Year _____

Day	Walking	Swimming	Jogging	Yoga	Stretching	Bicycling	Gardening	Resistance	Dancing	Golf	Tai Chi	Pickle Ball			Enjoyable
1															☹ 😃
2															☹ 😃
3															☹ 😃
4															☹ 😃
5															☹ 😃
6															☹ 😃
7															☹ 😃
8															☹ 😃
9															☹ 😃
10															☹ 😃
11															☹ 😃
12															☹ 😃
13															☹ 😃
14															☹ 😃
15															☹ 😃
16															☹ 😃
17															☹ 😃
18															☹ 😃
19															☹ 😃
20															☹ 😃
21															☹ 😃
22															☹ 😃
23															☹ 😃
24															☹ 😃
25															☹ 😃
26															☹ 😃
27															☹ 😃
28															☹ 😃
29															☹ 😃
30															☹ 😃
31															☹ 😃

DAILY ACTIVITY: SOCIAL LIFE

Month _____

Year _____

Day	Visit Friends	Eat Out	Volunteer	Class	Play Cards	Shopping	Sr. Center	Painting	Mall Walk	Babysit	Walk Dog				Enjoyable
1															☹ 🙂
2															☹ 🙂
3															☹ 🙂
4															☹ 🙂
5															☹ 🙂
6															☹ 🙂
7															☹ 🙂
8															☹ 🙂
9															☹ 🙂
10															☹ 🙂
11															☹ 🙂
12															☹ 🙂
13															☹ 🙂
14															☹ 🙂
15															☹ 🙂
16															☹ 🙂
17															☹ 🙂
18															☹ 🙂
19															☹ 🙂
20															☹ 🙂
21															☹ 🙂
22															☹ 🙂
23															☹ 🙂
24															☹ 🙂
25															☹ 🙂
26															☹ 🙂
27															☹ 🙂
28															☹ 🙂
29															☹ 🙂
30															☹ 🙂
31															☹ 🙂

DAILY ACTIVITY: FITNESS

Month _____

Year _____

Day	Walking	Swimming	Jogging	Yoga	Stretching	Bicycling	Gardening	Resistance	Dancing	Golf	Tai Chi	Pickle Ball			Enjoyable
1															😐 😃
2															😐 😃
3															😐 😃
4															😐 😃
5															😐 😃
6															😐 😃
7															😐 😃
8															😐 😃
9															😐 😃
10															😐 😃
11															😐 😃
12															😐 😃
13															😐 😃
14															😐 😃
15															😐 😃
16															😐 😃
17															😐 😃
18															😐 😃
19															😐 😃
20															😐 😃
21															😐 😃
22															😐 😃
23															😐 😃
24															😐 😃
25															😐 😃
26															😐 😃
27															😐 😃
28															😐 😃
29															😐 😃
30															😐 😃
31															😐 😃

DAILY ACTIVITY: SOCIAL LIFE

Month _____

Year _____

Day	Visit Friends	Eat Out	Volunteer	Class	Play Cards	Shopping	Sr. Center	Painting	Mall Walk	Babysit	Walk Dog				Enjoyable
1															☹ ☺
2															☹ ☺
3															☹ ☺
4															☹ ☺
5															☹ ☺
6															☹ ☺
7															☹ ☺
8															☹ ☺
9															☹ ☺
10															☹ ☺
11															☹ ☺
12															☹ ☺
13															☹ ☺
14															☹ ☺
15															☹ ☺
16															☹ ☺
17															☹ ☺
18															☹ ☺
19															☹ ☺
20															☹ ☺
21															☹ ☺
22															☹ ☺
23															☹ ☺
24															☹ ☺
25															☹ ☺
26															☹ ☺
27															☹ ☺
28															☹ ☺
29															☹ ☺
30															☹ ☺
31															☹ ☺

DAILY ACTIVITY: FITNESS

Month _____

Year _____

Day	Walking	Swimming	Jogging	Yoga	Stretching	Bicycling	Gardening	Resistance	Dancing	Golf	Tai Chi	Pickle Ball			Enjoyable
1															☹ 😃
2															☹ 😃
3															☹ 😃
4															☹ 😃
5															☹ 😃
6															☹ 😃
7															☹ 😃
8															☹ 😃
9															☹ 😃
10															☹ 😃
11															☹ 😃
12															☹ 😃
13															☹ 😃
14															☹ 😃
15															☹ 😃
16															☹ 😃
17															☹ 😃
18															☹ 😃
19															☹ 😃
20															☹ 😃
21															☹ 😃
22															☹ 😃
23															☹ 😃
24															☹ 😃
25															☹ 😃
26															☹ 😃
27															☹ 😃
28															☹ 😃
29															☹ 😃
30															☹ 😃
31															☹ 😃

DAILY ACTIVITY: SOCIAL LIFE

Month _____

Year _____

Day	Visit Friends	Eat Out	Volunteer	Class	Play Cards	Shopping	Sr. Center	Painting	Mall Walk	Babysit	Walk Dog				Enjoyable
1															☹ ☺
2															☹ ☺
3															☹ ☺
4															☹ ☺
5															☹ ☺
6															☹ ☺
7															☹ ☺
8															☹ ☺
9															☹ ☺
10															☹ ☺
11															☹ ☺
12															☹ ☺
13															☹ ☺
14															☹ ☺
15															☹ ☺
16															☹ ☺
17															☹ ☺
18															☹ ☺
19															☹ ☺
20															☹ ☺
21															☹ ☺
22															☹ ☺
23															☹ ☺
24															☹ ☺
25															☹ ☺
26															☹ ☺
27															☹ ☺
28															☹ ☺
29															☹ ☺
30															☹ ☺
31															☹ ☺

DAILY ACTIVITY: FITNESS

Month _____

Year _____

Day	Walking	Swimming	Jogging	Yoga	Stretching	Bicycling	Gardening	Resistance	Dancing	Golf	Tai Chi	Pickle Ball		Enjoyable
1														😐 😃
2														😐 😃
3														😐 😃
4														😐 😃
5														😐 😃
6														😐 😃
7														😐 😃
8														😐 😃
9														😐 😃
10														😐 😃
11														😐 😃
12														😐 😃
13														😐 😃
14														😐 😃
15														😐 😃
16														😐 😃
17														😐 😃
18														😐 😃
19														😐 😃
20														😐 😃
21														😐 😃
22														😐 😃
23														😐 😃
24														😐 😃
25														😐 😃
26														😐 😃
27														😐 😃
28														😐 😃
29														😐 😃
30														😐 😃
31														😐 😃

DAILY ACTIVITY: SOCIAL LIFE

Month _____

Year _____

Day	Visit Friends	Eat Out	Volunteer	Class	Play Cards	Shopping	Sr. Center	Painting	Mall Walk	Babysit	Walk Dog				Enjoyable
1															🙁 🙂
2															🙁 🙂
3															🙁 🙂
4															🙁 🙂
5															🙁 🙂
6															🙁 🙂
7															🙁 🙂
8															🙁 🙂
9															🙁 🙂
10															🙁 🙂
11															🙁 🙂
12															🙁 🙂
13															🙁 🙂
14															🙁 🙂
15															🙁 🙂
16															🙁 🙂
17															🙁 🙂
18															🙁 🙂
19															🙁 🙂
20															🙁 🙂
21															🙁 🙂
22															🙁 🙂
23															🙁 🙂
24															🙁 🙂
25															🙁 🙂
26															🙁 🙂
27															🙁 🙂
28															🙁 🙂
29															🙁 🙂
30															🙁 🙂
31															🙁 🙂

DAILY ACTIVITY: FITNESS

Month _____

Year _____

Day	Walking	Swimming	Jogging	Yoga	Stretching	Bicycling	Gardening	Resistance	Dancing	Golf	Tai Chi	Pickle Ball			Enjoyable
1															☹ 😃
2															☹ 😃
3															☹ 😃
4															☹ 😃
5															☹ 😃
6															☹ 😃
7															☹ 😃
8															☹ 😃
9															☹ 😃
10															☹ 😃
11															☹ 😃
12															☹ 😃
13															☹ 😃
14															☹ 😃
15															☹ 😃
16															☹ 😃
17															☹ 😃
18															☹ 😃
19															☹ 😃
20															☹ 😃
21															☹ 😃
22															☹ 😃
23															☹ 😃
24															☹ 😃
25															☹ 😃
26															☹ 😃
27															☹ 😃
28															☹ 😃
29															☹ 😃
30															☹ 😃
31															☹ 😃

DAILY ACTIVITY: SOCIAL LIFE

Month _____

Year _____

Day	Visit Friends	Eat Out	Volunteer	Class	Play Cards	Shopping	Sr. Center	Painting	Mall Walk	Babysit	Walk Dog				Enjoyable
1															☹ ☺
2															☹ ☺
3															☹ ☺
4															☹ ☺
5															☹ ☺
6															☹ ☺
7															☹ ☺
8															☹ ☺
9															☹ ☺
10															☹ ☺
11															☹ ☺
12															☹ ☺
13															☹ ☺
14															☹ ☺
15															☹ ☺
16															☹ ☺
17															☹ ☺
18															☹ ☺
19															☹ ☺
20															☹ ☺
21															☹ ☺
22															☹ ☺
23															☹ ☺
24															☹ ☺
25															☹ ☺
26															☹ ☺
27															☹ ☺
28															☹ ☺
29															☹ ☺
30															☹ ☺
31															☹ ☺

DAILY ACTIVITY: FITNESS

Month _____

Year _____

Day	Walking	Swimming	Jogging	Yoga	Stretching	Bicycling	Gardening	Resistance	Dancing	Golf	Tai Chi	Pickle Ball		Enjoyable
1														☹ 😃
2														☹ 😃
3														☹ 😃
4														☹ 😃
5														☹ 😃
6														☹ 😃
7														☹ 😃
8														☹ 😃
9														☹ 😃
10														☹ 😃
11														☹ 😃
12														☹ 😃
13														☹ 😃
14														☹ 😃
15														☹ 😃
16														☹ 😃
17														☹ 😃
18														☹ 😃
19														☹ 😃
20														☹ 😃
21														☹ 😃
22														☹ 😃
23														☹ 😃
24														☹ 😃
25														☹ 😃
26														☹ 😃
27														☹ 😃
28														☹ 😃
29														☹ 😃
30														☹ 😃
31														☹ 😃

DAILY ACTIVITY: SOCIAL LIFE

Month _____

Year _____

Day	Visit Friends	Eat Out	Volunteer	Class	Play Cards	Shopping	Sr. Center	Painting	Mall Walk	Babysit	Walk Dog				Enjoyable
1															☹ 😊
2															☹ 😊
3															☹ 😊
4															☹ 😊
5															☹ 😊
6															☹ 😊
7															☹ 😊
8															☹ 😊
9															☹ 😊
10															☹ 😊
11															☹ 😊
12															☹ 😊
13															☹ 😊
14															☹ 😊
15															☹ 😊
16															☹ 😊
17															☹ 😊
18															☹ 😊
19															☹ 😊
20															☹ 😊
21															☹ 😊
22															☹ 😊
23															☹ 😊
24															☹ 😊
25															☹ 😊
26															☹ 😊
27															☹ 😊
28															☹ 😊
29															☹ 😊
30															☹ 😊
31															☹ 😊

DAILY ACTIVITY: FITNESS

Month _____

Year _____

Day	Walking	Swimming	Jogging	Yoga	Stretching	Bicycling	Gardening	Resistance	Dancing	Golf	Tai Chi	Pickle Ball		Enjoyable
1														☹ 😃
2														☹ 😃
3														☹ 😃
4														☹ 😃
5														☹ 😃
6														☹ 😃
7														☹ 😃
8														☹ 😃
9														☹ 😃
10														☹ 😃
11														☹ 😃
12														☹ 😃
13														☹ 😃
14														☹ 😃
15														☹ 😃
16														☹ 😃
17														☹ 😃
18														☹ 😃
19														☹ 😃
20														☹ 😃
21														☹ 😃
22														☹ 😃
23														☹ 😃
24														☹ 😃
25														☹ 😃
26														☹ 😃
27														☹ 😃
28														☹ 😃
29														☹ 😃
30														☹ 😃
31														☹ 😃

DAILY ACTIVITY: SOCIAL LIFE

Month _____

Year _____

Day	Visit Friends	Eat Out	Volunteer	Class	Play Cards	Shopping	Sr. Center	Painting	Mall Walk	Babysit	Walk Dog				Enjoyable
1															☹ ☺
2															☹ ☺
3															☹ ☺
4															☹ ☺
5															☹ ☺
6															☹ ☺
7															☹ ☺
8															☹ ☺
9															☹ ☺
10															☹ ☺
11															☹ ☺
12															☹ ☺
13															☹ ☺
14															☹ ☺
15															☹ ☺
16															☹ ☺
17															☹ ☺
18															☹ ☺
19															☹ ☺
20															☹ ☺
21															☹ ☺
22															☹ ☺
23															☹ ☺
24															☹ ☺
25															☹ ☺
26															☹ ☺
27															☹ ☺
28															☹ ☺
29															☹ ☺
30															☹ ☺
31															☹ ☺

DAILY ACTIVITY: FITNESS

Month _____

Year _____

Day	Walking	Swimming	Jogging	Yoga	Stretching	Bicycling	Gardening	Resistance	Dancing	Golf	Tai Chi	Pickle Ball		Enjoyable
1														😐 😃
2														😐 😃
3														😐 😃
4														😐 😃
5														😐 😃
6														😐 😃
7														😐 😃
8														😐 😃
9														😐 😃
10														😐 😃
11														😐 😃
12														😐 😃
13														😐 😃
14														😐 😃
15														😐 😃
16														😐 😃
17														😐 😃
18														😐 😃
19														😐 😃
20														😐 😃
21														😐 😃
22														😐 😃
23														😐 😃
24														😐 😃
25														😐 😃
26														😐 😃
27														😐 😃
28														😐 😃
29														😐 😃
30														😐 😃
31														😐 😃

DAILY ACTIVITY: SOCIAL LIFE

Month _____

Year _____

Day	Visit Friends	Eat Out	Volunteer	Class	Play Cards	Shopping	Sr. Center	Painting	Mall Walk	Babysit	Walk Dog				Enjoyable
1															☹ ☺
2															☹ ☺
3															☹ ☺
4															☹ ☺
5															☹ ☺
6															☹ ☺
7															☹ ☺
8															☹ ☺
9															☹ ☺
10															☹ ☺
11															☹ ☺
12															☹ ☺
13															☹ ☺
14															☹ ☺
15															☹ ☺
16															☹ ☺
17															☹ ☺
18															☹ ☺
19															☹ ☺
20															☹ ☺
21															☹ ☺
22															☹ ☺
23															☹ ☺
24															☹ ☺
25															☹ ☺
26															☹ ☺
27															☹ ☺
28															☹ ☺
29															☹ ☺
30															☹ ☺
31															☹ ☺

DAILY ACTIVITY: FITNESS

Month _____

Year _____

Day	Walking	Swimming	Jogging	Yoga	Stretching	Bicycling	Gardening	Resistance	Dancing	Golf	Tai Chi	Pickle Ball		Enjoyable
1														☹ 😃
2														☹ 😃
3														☹ 😃
4														☹ 😃
5														☹ 😃
6														☹ 😃
7														☹ 😃
8														☹ 😃
9														☹ 😃
10														☹ 😃
11														☹ 😃
12														☹ 😃
13														☹ 😃
14														☹ 😃
15														☹ 😃
16														☹ 😃
17														☹ 😃
18														☹ 😃
19														☹ 😃
20														☹ 😃
21														☹ 😃
22														☹ 😃
23														☹ 😃
24														☹ 😃
25														☹ 😃
26														☹ 😃
27														☹ 😃
28														☹ 😃
29														☹ 😃
30														☹ 😃
31														☹ 😃

DAILY ACTIVITY: SOCIAL LIFE

Month_____

Year_____

Day	Visit Friends	Eat Out	Volunteer	Class	Play Cards	Shopping	Sr. Center	Painting	Mall Walk	Babysit	Walk Dog				Enjoyable
1															☹ ☺
2															☹ ☺
3															☹ ☺
4															☹ ☺
5															☹ ☺
6															☹ ☺
7															☹ ☺
8															☹ ☺
9															☹ ☺
10															☹ ☺
11															☹ ☺
12															☹ ☺
13															☹ ☺
14															☹ ☺
15															☹ ☺
16															☹ ☺
17															☹ ☺
18															☹ ☺
19															☹ ☺
20															☹ ☺
21															☹ ☺
22															☹ ☺
23															☹ ☺
24															☹ ☺
25															☹ ☺
26															☹ ☺
27															☹ ☺
28															☹ ☺
29															☹ ☺
30															☹ ☺
31															☹ ☺

DAILY FITNESS & ACTIVITY JOURNAL

Date	Today's Goal		
☐ Walking ☐ Jogging	☐ Yoga ☐ Swim	☐ Bicycle/Spin ☐ Meditation	☐ Aerobics ☐ Weights/Balance
Group Activity?		Exercise Duration	
Step Count		Distance	

Notes and Observations:

DAILY FITNESS & ACTIVITY JOURNAL

Date	Today's Goal		
☐ Walking ☐ Jogging	☐ Yoga ☐ Swim	☐ Bicycle/Spin ☐ Meditation	☐ Aerobics ☐ Weights/Balance
Group Activity?		Exercise Duration	
Step Count		Distance	

Notes and Observations:

DAILY FITNESS & ACTIVITY JOURNAL

Date	Today's Goal		
☐ Walking ☐ Jogging	☐ Yoga ☐ Swim	☐ Bicycle/Spin ☐ Meditation	☐ Aerobics ☐ Weights/Balance
Group Activity?		Exercise Duration	
Step Count		Distance	

Notes and Observations:

DAILY FITNESS & ACTIVITY JOURNAL

Date	Today's Goal		
☐ Walking ☐ Jogging	☐ Yoga ☐ Swim	☐ Bicycle/Spin ☐ Meditation	☐ Aerobics ☐ Weights/Balance
Group Activity?		Exercise Duration	
Step Count		Distance	

Notes and Observations:

DAILY FITNESS & ACTIVITY JOURNAL

Date	Today's Goal		
☐ Walking ☐ Jogging	☐ Yoga ☐ Swim	☐ Bicycle/Spin ☐ Meditation	☐ Aerobics ☐ Weights/Balance
Group Activity?		Exercise Duration	
Step Count		Distance	

Notes and Observations:

DAILY FITNESS & ACTIVITY JOURNAL

Date	Today's Goal		
☐ Walking ☐ Jogging	☐ Yoga ☐ Swim	☐ Bicycle/Spin ☐ Meditation	☐ Aerobics ☐ Weights/Balance
Group Activity?		Exercise Duration	
Step Count		Distance	

Notes and Observations:

DAILY FITNESS & ACTIVITY JOURNAL

Date	Today's Goal		
☐ Walking ☐ Jogging	☐ Yoga ☐ Swim	☐ Bicycle/Spin ☐ Meditation	☐ Aerobics ☐ Weights/Balance
Group Activity?		Exercise Duration	
Step Count		Distance	

Notes and Observations:

DAILY FITNESS & ACTIVITY JOURNAL

Date	Today's Goal		
☐ Walking ☐ Jogging	☐ Yoga ☐ Swim	☐ Bicycle/Spin ☐ Meditation	☐ Aerobics ☐ Weights/Balance
Group Activity?		Exercise Duration	
Step Count		Distance	

Notes and Observations:

DAILY FITNESS & ACTIVITY JOURNAL

Date	Today's Goal		
☐ Walking ☐ Jogging	☐ Yoga ☐ Swim	☐ Bicycle/Spin ☐ Meditation	☐ Aerobics ☐ Weights/Balance
Group Activity?		Exercise Duration	
Step Count		Distance	

Notes and Observations:

DAILY FITNESS & ACTIVITY JOURNAL

Date	Today's Goal		
☐ Walking ☐ Jogging	☐ Yoga ☐ Swim	☐ Bicycle/Spin ☐ Meditation	☐ Aerobics ☐ Weights/Balance
Group Activity?		Exercise Duration	
Step Count		Distance	

Notes and Observations:

DAILY FITNESS & ACTIVITY JOURNAL

Date	Today's Goal		
☐ Walking ☐ Jogging	☐ Yoga ☐ Swim	☐ Bicycle/Spin ☐ Meditation	☐ Aerobics ☐ Weights/Balance
Group Activity?		Exercise Duration	
Step Count		Distance	

Notes and Observations:

DAILY FITNESS & ACTIVITY JOURNAL

Date	Today's Goal		
☐ Walking ☐ Jogging	☐ Yoga ☐ Swim	☐ Bicycle/Spin ☐ Meditation	☐ Aerobics ☐ Weights/Balance
Group Activity?		Exercise Duration	
Step Count		Distance	

Notes and Observations:

DAILY FITNESS & ACTIVITY JOURNAL

Date	Today's Goal		
☐ Walking ☐ Jogging	☐ Yoga ☐ Swim	☐ Bicycle/Spin ☐ Meditation	☐ Aerobics ☐ Weights/Balance
Group Activity?		Exercise Duration	
Step Count		Distance	

Notes and Observations:

DAILY FITNESS & ACTIVITY JOURNAL

Date	Today's Goal		
☐ Walking ☐ Jogging	☐ Yoga ☐ Swim	☐ Bicycle/Spin ☐ Meditation	☐ Aerobics ☐ Weights/Balance
Group Activity?		Exercise Duration	
Step Count		Distance	

Notes and Observations:

DAILY FITNESS & ACTIVITY JOURNAL

Date	Today's Goal		
☐ Walking ☐ Jogging	☐ Yoga ☐ Swim	☐ Bicycle/Spin ☐ Meditation	☐ Aerobics ☐ Weights/Balance
Group Activity?		Exercise Duration	
Step Count		Distance	

Notes and Observations:

DAILY FITNESS & ACTIVITY JOURNAL

Date	Today's Goal		
☐ Walking ☐ Jogging	☐ Yoga ☐ Swim	☐ Bicycle/Spin ☐ Meditation	☐ Aerobics ☐ Weights/Balance
Group Activity?		Exercise Duration	
Step Count		Distance	

Notes and Observations:

DAILY FITNESS & ACTIVITY JOURNAL

Date	Today's Goal		
☐ Walking ☐ Jogging	☐ Yoga ☐ Swim	☐ Bicycle/Spin ☐ Meditation	☐ Aerobics ☐ Weights/Balance
Group Activity?		Exercise Duration	
Step Count		Distance	

Notes and Observations:

DAILY FITNESS & ACTIVITY JOURNAL

Date	Today's Goal		
☐ Walking ☐ Jogging	☐ Yoga ☐ Swim	☐ Bicycle/Spin ☐ Meditation	☐ Aerobics ☐ Weights/Balance
Group Activity?		Exercise Duration	
Step Count		Distance	

Notes and Observations:

DAILY FITNESS & ACTIVITY JOURNAL

Date	Today's Goal		
☐ Walking ☐ Jogging	☐ Yoga ☐ Swim	☐ Bicycle/Spin ☐ Meditation	☐ Aerobics ☐ Weights/Balance
Group Activity?		Exercise Duration	
Step Count		Distance	

Notes and Observations:

DAILY FITNESS & ACTIVITY JOURNAL

Date	Today's Goal		
☐ Walking ☐ Jogging	☐ Yoga ☐ Swim	☐ Bicycle/Spin ☐ Meditation	☐ Aerobics ☐ Weights/Balance
Group Activity?		Exercise Duration	
Step Count		Distance	

Notes and Observations:

DAILY FITNESS & ACTIVITY JOURNAL

Date	Today's Goal		
☐ Walking ☐ Jogging	☐ Yoga ☐ Swim	☐ Bicycle/Spin ☐ Meditation	☐ Aerobics ☐ Weights/Balance
Group Activity?		Exercise Duration	
Step Count		Distance	

Notes and Observations:

DAILY FITNESS & ACTIVITY JOURNAL

Date	Today's Goal		
☐ Walking ☐ Jogging	☐ Yoga ☐ Swim	☐ Bicycle/Spin ☐ Meditation	☐ Aerobics ☐ Weights/Balance
Group Activity?		Exercise Duration	
Step Count		Distance	

Notes and Observations:

DAILY FITNESS & ACTIVITY JOURNAL

Date	Today's Goal		
☐ Walking ☐ Jogging	☐ Yoga ☐ Swim	☐ Bicycle/Spin ☐ Meditation	☐ Aerobics ☐ Weights/Balance
Group Activity?		Exercise Duration	
Step Count		Distance	

Notes and Observations:

DAILY FITNESS & ACTIVITY JOURNAL

Date	Today's Goal		
☐ Walking ☐ Jogging	☐ Yoga ☐ Swim	☐ Bicycle/Spin ☐ Meditation	☐ Aerobics ☐ Weights/Balance
Group Activity?		Exercise Duration	
Step Count		Distance	

Notes and Observations:

DAILY FITNESS & ACTIVITY JOURNAL

Date	Today's Goal		
☐ Walking ☐ Jogging	☐ Yoga ☐ Swim	☐ Bicycle/Spin ☐ Meditation	☐ Aerobics ☐ Weights/Balance
Group Activity?		Exercise Duration	
Step Count		Distance	

Notes and Observations:

DAILY FITNESS & ACTIVITY JOURNAL

Date	Today's Goal		
☐ Walking ☐ Jogging	☐ Yoga ☐ Swim	☐ Bicycle/Spin ☐ Meditation	☐ Aerobics ☐ Weights/Balance
Group Activity?		Exercise Duration	
Step Count		Distance	

Notes and Observations:

DAILY FITNESS & ACTIVITY JOURNAL

Date	Today's Goal		
☐ Walking ☐ Jogging	☐ Yoga ☐ Swim	☐ Bicycle/Spin ☐ Meditation	☐ Aerobics ☐ Weights/Balance
Group Activity?		Exercise Duration	
Step Count		Distance	

Notes and Observations:

DAILY FITNESS & ACTIVITY JOURNAL

Date	Today's Goal		
☐ Walking ☐ Jogging	☐ Yoga ☐ Swim	☐ Bicycle/Spin ☐ Meditation	☐ Aerobics ☐ Weights/Balance
Group Activity?		Exercise Duration	
Step Count		Distance	

Notes and Observations:

DAILY FITNESS & ACTIVITY JOURNAL

Date	Today's Goal		
☐ Walking ☐ Jogging	☐ Yoga ☐ Swim	☐ Bicycle/Spin ☐ Meditation	☐ Aerobics ☐ Weights/Balance
Group Activity?		Exercise Duration	
Step Count		Distance	

Notes and Observations:

DAILY FITNESS & ACTIVITY JOURNAL

Date	Today's Goal		
☐ Walking ☐ Jogging	☐ Yoga ☐ Swim	☐ Bicycle/Spin ☐ Meditation	☐ Aerobics ☐ Weights/Balance
Group Activity?		Exercise Duration	
Step Count		Distance	

Notes and Observations:

Achievements & Goals

Clubs, Classes & Hobbies

NEW HABITS to MAKE

OLD HABITS to BREAK

Daily Accomplishments, Affirmations, Goals

Month: _____

1	
2	
3	
4	
5	
6	
7	
8	
9	
10	
11	
12	
13	
14	
15	
16	

Notes:

Daily Accomplishments, Affirmations, Goals

Month: _____

17	
18	
19	
20	
21	
22	
23	
24	
25	
26	
27	
28	
29	
30	
31	

Notes:

Daily Accomplishments, Affirmations, Goals

Month: _____

1	
2	
3	
4	
5	
6	
7	
8	
9	
10	
11	
12	
13	
14	
15	
16	

Notes:

Daily Accomplishments, Affirmations, Goals

Month: _____

17	
18	
19	
20	
21	
22	
23	
24	
25	
26	
27	
28	
29	
30	
31	

Notes:

Daily Accomplishments, Affirmations, Goals

Month: _____

1	
2	
3	
4	
5	
6	
7	
8	
9	
10	
11	
12	
13	
14	
15	
16	

Notes:

Daily Accomplishments, Affirmations, Goals

Month: _____

17	
18	
19	
20	
21	
22	
23	
24	
25	
26	
27	
28	
29	
30	
31	

Notes:

Daily Accomplishments, Affirmations, Goals

Month: _____

1	
2	
3	
4	
5	
6	
7	
8	
9	
10	
11	
12	
13	
14	
15	
16	

Notes:

Daily Accomplishments, Affirmations, Goals

Month: _____

17	
18	
19	
20	
21	
22	
23	
24	
25	
26	
27	
28	
29	
30	
31	

Notes:

Daily Accomplishments, Affirmations, Goals

Month: _____

1	
2	
3	
4	
5	
6	
7	
8	
9	
10	
11	
12	
13	
14	
15	
16	

Notes:

Daily Accomplishments, Affirmations, Goals

Month: _____

17	
18	
19	
20	
21	
22	
23	
24	
25	
26	
27	
28	
29	
30	
31	

Notes:

Daily Accomplishments, Affirmations, Goals

Month: _____

1	
2	
3	
4	
5	
6	
7	
8	
9	
10	
11	
12	
13	
14	
15	
16	

Notes:

Daily Accomplishments, Affirmations, Goals

Month: _____

17	
18	
19	
20	
21	
22	
23	
24	
25	
26	
27	
28	
29	
30	
31	

Notes:

Daily Accomplishments, Affirmations, Goals

Month: _____

1	
2	
3	
4	
5	
6	
7	
8	
9	
10	
11	
12	
13	
14	
15	
16	

Notes:

Daily Accomplishments, Affirmations, Goals

Month: _____

17	
18	
19	
20	
21	
22	
23	
24	
25	
26	
27	
28	
29	
30	
31	

Notes:

Daily Accomplishments, Affirmations, Goals

Month: _____

1	
2	
3	
4	
5	
6	
7	
8	
9	
10	
11	
12	
13	
14	
15	
16	

Notes:

Daily Accomplishments, Affirmations, Goals

Month: _____

17	
18	
19	
20	
21	
22	
23	
24	
25	
26	
27	
28	
29	
30	
31	

Notes:

Daily Accomplishments, Affirmations, Goals

Month: _____

1	
2	
3	
4	
5	
6	
7	
8	
9	
10	
11	
12	
13	
14	
15	
16	

Notes:

Daily Accomplishments, Affirmations, Goals

Month: _____

17	
18	
19	
20	
21	
22	
23	
24	
25	
26	
27	
28	
29	
30	
31	

Notes:

Daily Accomplishments, Affirmations, Goals

Month: _____

1	
2	
3	
4	
5	
6	
7	
8	
9	
10	
11	
12	
13	
14	
15	
16	

Notes:

Daily Accomplishments, Affirmations, Goals

Month: _____

17	
18	
19	
20	
21	
22	
23	
24	
25	
26	
27	
28	
29	
30	
31	

Notes:

Daily Accomplishments, Affirmations, Goals

Month: _____

1	
2	
3	
4	
5	
6	
7	
8	
9	
10	
11	
12	
13	
14	
15	
16	

Notes:

Daily Accomplishments, Affirmations, Goals

Month: _____

17	
18	
19	
20	
21	
22	
23	
24	
25	
26	
27	
28	
29	
30	
31	

Notes:

Daily Accomplishments, Affirmations, Goals

Month: _____

1	
2	
3	
4	
5	
6	
7	
8	
9	
10	
11	
12	
13	
14	
15	
16	

Notes:

Daily Accomplishments, Affirmations, Goals

Month: _____

17	
18	
19	
20	
21	
22	
23	
24	
25	
26	
27	
28	
29	
30	
31	

Notes:

New Skills I Want to Learn

Classes, Clubs, Meetings, Hobbies

An Achievement to Celebrate:

Classes, Clubs, Meetings, Hobbies

An Achievement to Celebrate:

Classes, Clubs, Meetings, Hobbies

An Achievement to Celebrate:

Classes, Clubs, Meetings, Hobbies

An Achievement to Celebrate:

The most beautiful sunset I've seen this year

The most beautiful flower I've seen this year

The most fun I've had this year

The best meal I've eaten this year

The best book I've ever read

My favorite movie is & why ...

The best vacation I've taken

The one place I'd most like to visit

The person (real, fictional, alive, or dead) I'd like to have coffee with

This makes me peaceful and calm

The thing that makes me most proud

What I'm looking forward to doing next

Personal & Medical

Info & Contacts

What Affects My Mood

Date	Weather	Notes	Mood
			😐 😔 😮 🙂 😁
			😐 😔 😮 🙂 😁
			😐 😔 😮 🙂 😁
			😐 😔 😮 🙂 😁
			😐 😔 😮 🙂 😁
			😐 😔 😮 🙂 😁
			😐 😔 😮 🙂 😁
			😐 😔 😮 🙂 😁
			😐 😔 😮 🙂 😁
			😐 😔 😮 🙂 😁
			😐 😔 😮 🙂 😁
			😐 😔 😮 🙂 😁
			😐 😔 😮 🙂 😁
			😐 😔 😮 🙂 😁
			😐 😔 😮 🙂 😁
			😐 😔 😮 🙂 😁
			😐 😔 😮 🙂 😁
			😐 😔 😮 🙂 😁
			😐 😔 😮 🙂 😁
			😐 😔 😮 🙂 😁

MEDICAL PROVIDERS

Insurance Provider _____

Member Number _____

Primary Care Provider _____

Office Address _____

_____

City _____ State _____ Zip _____

Office Phone _____ Fax _____

Specialist _____

Specialty _____

Office Address _____

_____

City _____ State _____ Zip _____

Office Phone _____ Fax _____

Specialist _____

Specialty _____

Office Address _____

_____

City _____ State _____ Zip _____

Office Phone _____ Fax _____

| Specialist _____ |
| Specialty _____ |
| Office Address _____ |
| _____ |
| City _____ State _____ Zip _____ |
| Office Phone _____ Fax _____ |

| Specialist _____ |
| Specialty _____ |
| Office Address _____ |
| _____ |
| City _____ State _____ Zip _____ |
| Office Phone _____ Fax _____ |

| Specialist _____ |
| Specialty _____ |
| Office Address _____ |
| _____ |
| City _____ State _____ Zip _____ |
| Office Phone _____ Fax _____ |

Specialist _____

Specialty _____

Office Address _____

_____

City _____ State _____ Zip _____

Office Phone _____ Fax _____

MEDICATION

Preferred Pharmacy _____
☐ Local Pharmacy   ☐ Mail Order
Location _____
_____

City _____ State _____ Zip _____
Phone _____ Fax _____

Medication _____
Treatment for _____
☐ Generic   ☐ Over the Counter   ☐ Tier 1   ☐ Tier 2   ☐ Tier 3   ☐ Not Covered
Days Supply: ☐ 30 Days   ☐ 60 Days   ☐ 90 Days
Dosage _____ Every _____ Hours   ☐ Daily

Medication _____
Treatment for _____
☐ Generic   ☐ Over the Counter   ☐ Tier 1   ☐ Tier 2   ☐ Tier 3   ☐ Not Covered
Days Supply: ☐ 30 Days   ☐ 60 Days   ☐ 90 Days
Dosage _____ Every _____ Hours   ☐ Daily

Medication _____
Treatment for _____
☐ Generic   ☐ Over the Counter   ☐ Tier 1   ☐ Tier 2   ☐ Tier 3   ☐ Not Covered
Days Supply: ☐ 30 Days   ☐ 60 Days   ☐ 90 Days
Dosage _____ Every _____ Hours   ☐ Daily

MEDICATION

Medication _____

Treatment for _____

☐ Generic ☐ Over the Counter   ☐ Tier 1 ☐ Tier 2 ☐ Tier 3   ☐ Not Covered

Days Supply: ☐ 30 Days ☐ 60 Days ☐ 90 Days

Dosage _____   Every _____ Hours   ☐ Daily

Medication _____

Treatment for _____

☐ Generic ☐ Over the Counter   ☐ Tier 1 ☐ Tier 2 ☐ Tier 3   ☐ Not Covered

Days Supply: ☐ 30 Days ☐ 60 Days ☐ 90 Days

Dosage _____   Every _____ Hours   ☐ Daily

Medication _____

Treatment for _____

☐ Generic ☐ Over the Counter   ☐ Tier 1 ☐ Tier 2 ☐ Tier 3   ☐ Not Covered

Days Supply: ☐ 30 Days ☐ 60 Days ☐ 90 Days

Dosage _____   Every _____ Hours   ☐ Daily

Medication _____

Treatment for _____

☐ Generic ☐ Over the Counter   ☐ Tier 1 ☐ Tier 2 ☐ Tier 3   ☐ Not Covered

Days Supply: ☐ 30 Days ☐ 60 Days ☐ 90 Days

Dosage _____   Every _____ Hours   ☐ Daily

MEDICATION

Medication _____

Treatment for _____

☐ Generic ☐ Over the Counter   ☐ Tier 1 ☐ Tier 2 ☐ Tier 3   ☐ Not Covered

Days Supply: ☐ 30 Days ☐ 60 Days ☐ 90 Days

Dosage _____   Every _____ Hours   ☐ Daily

Medication _____

Treatment for _____

☐ Generic ☐ Over the Counter   ☐ Tier 1 ☐ Tier 2 ☐ Tier 3   ☐ Not Covered

Days Supply: ☐ 30 Days ☐ 60 Days ☐ 90 Days

Dosage _____   Every _____ Hours   ☐ Daily

Medication _____

Treatment for _____

☐ Generic ☐ Over the Counter   ☐ Tier 1 ☐ Tier 2 ☐ Tier 3   ☐ Not Covered

Days Supply: ☐ 30 Days ☐ 60 Days ☐ 90 Days

Dosage _____   Every _____ Hours   ☐ Daily

Medication _____

Treatment for _____

☐ Generic ☐ Over the Counter   ☐ Tier 1 ☐ Tier 2 ☐ Tier 3   ☐ Not Covered

Days Supply: ☐ 30 Days ☐ 60 Days ☐ 90 Days

Dosage _____   Every _____ Hours   ☐ Daily

MEDICATION

Medication _____

Treatment for _____

☐ Generic ☐ Over the Counter   ☐ Tier 1 ☐ Tier 2 ☐ Tier 3   ☐ Not Covered

Days Supply: ☐ 30 Days ☐ 60 Days ☐ 90 Days

Dosage _____   Every _____ Hours   ☐ Daily

Medication _____

Treatment for _____

☐ Generic ☐ Over the Counter   ☐ Tier 1 ☐ Tier 2 ☐ Tier 3   ☐ Not Covered

Days Supply: ☐ 30 Days ☐ 60 Days ☐ 90 Days

Dosage _____   Every _____ Hours   ☐ Daily

Medication _____

Treatment for _____

☐ Generic ☐ Over the Counter   ☐ Tier 1 ☐ Tier 2 ☐ Tier 3   ☐ Not Covered

Days Supply: ☐ 30 Days ☐ 60 Days ☐ 90 Days

Dosage _____   Every _____ Hours   ☐ Daily

Medication _____

Treatment for _____

☐ Generic ☐ Over the Counter   ☐ Tier 1 ☐ Tier 2 ☐ Tier 3   ☐ Not Covered

Days Supply: ☐ 30 Days ☐ 60 Days ☐ 90 Days

Dosage _____   Every _____ Hours   ☐ Daily

HEALTH & VITALS

Month _____

Year _____

Day	Heart Rate	Blood O2	Blood Pressure over	Blood Pressure	Weight	Temperature	Blood Glucose	Number of Falls	Inhaler Usage	Bruising?	Joint Pain?				Sleep Well
1															😐 😃
2															😐 😃
3															😐 😃
4															😐 😃
5															😐 😃
6															😐 😃
7															😐 😃
8															😐 😃
9															😐 😃
10															😐 😃
11															😐 😃
12															😐 😃
13															😐 😃
14															😐 😃
15															😐 😃
16															😐 😃
17															😐 😃
18															😐 😃
19															😐 😃
20															😐 😃
21															😐 😃
22															😐 😃
23															😐 😃
24															😐 😃
25															😐 😃
26															😐 😃
27															😐 😃
28															😐 😃
29															😐 😃
30															😐 😃
31															😐 😃

HEALTH & VITALS

Month_____

Year _____

Day	Heart Rate	Blood O2	Blood Pressure over	Blood Pressure	Weight	Temperature	Blood Glucose	Number of Falls	Inhaler Usage	Bruising?	Joint Pain?				Sleep Well
1															😐 😊
2															😐 😊
3															😐 😊
4															😐 😊
5															😐 😊
6															😐 😊
7															😐 😊
8															😐 😊
9															😐 😊
10															😐 😊
11															😐 😊
12															😐 😊
13															😐 😊
14															😐 😊
15															😐 😊
16															😐 😊
17															😐 😊
18															😐 😊
19															😐 😊
20															😐 😊
21															😐 😊
22															😐 😊
23															😐 😊
24															😐 😊
25															😐 😊
26															😐 😊
27															😐 😊
28															😐 😊
29															😐 😊
30															😐 😊
31															😐 😊

HEALTH & VITALS

Month _____

Year _____

Day	Heart Rate	Blood O2	Blood Pressure over	Blood Pressure	Weight	Temperature	Blood Glucose	Number of Falls	Inhaler Usage	Bruising?	Joint Pain?				Sleep Well
1															☹ 🙂
2															☹ 🙂
3															☹ 🙂
4															☹ 🙂
5															☹ 🙂
6															☹ 🙂
7															☹ 🙂
8															☹ 🙂
9															☹ 🙂
10															☹ 🙂
11															☹ 🙂
12															☹ 🙂
13															☹ 🙂
14															☹ 🙂
15															☹ 🙂
16															☹ 🙂
17															☹ 🙂
18															☹ 🙂
19															☹ 🙂
20															☹ 🙂
21															☹ 🙂
22															☹ 🙂
23															☹ 🙂
24															☹ 🙂
25															☹ 🙂
26															☹ 🙂
27															☹ 🙂
28															☹ 🙂
29															☹ 🙂
30															☹ 🙂
31															☹ 🙂

HEALTH & VITALS

Month_____

Year_____

Day	Heart Rate	Blood O2	Blood Pressure over	Blood Pressure	Weight	Temperature	Blood Glucose	Number of Falls	Inhaler Usage	Bruising?	Joint Pain?				Sleep Well
1															☹ ☺
2															☹ ☺
3															☹ ☺
4															☹ ☺
5															☹ ☺
6															☹ ☺
7															☹ ☺
8															☹ ☺
9															☹ ☺
10															☹ ☺
11															☹ ☺
12															☹ ☺
13															☹ ☺
14															☹ ☺
15															☹ ☺
16															☹ ☺
17															☹ ☺
18															☹ ☺
19															☹ ☺
20															☹ ☺
21															☹ ☺
22															☹ ☺
23															☹ ☺
24															☹ ☺
25															☹ ☺
26															☹ ☺
27															☹ ☺
28															☹ ☺
29															☹ ☺
30															☹ ☺
31															☹ ☺

HEALTH & VITALS

Month _____

Year _____

Day	Heart Rate	Blood O2	Blood Pressure over	Blood Pressure	Weight	Temperature	Blood Glucose	Number of Falls	Inhaler Usage	Bruising?	Joint Pain?				Sleep Well
1															☹ 🙂
2															☹ 🙂
3															☹ 🙂
4															☹ 🙂
5															☹ 🙂
6															☹ 🙂
7															☹ 🙂
8															☹ 🙂
9															☹ 🙂
10															☹ 🙂
11															☹ 🙂
12															☹ 🙂
13															☹ 🙂
14															☹ 🙂
15															☹ 🙂
16															☹ 🙂
17															☹ 🙂
18															☹ 🙂
19															☹ 🙂
20															☹ 🙂
21															☹ 🙂
22															☹ 🙂
23															☹ 🙂
24															☹ 🙂
25															☹ 🙂
26															☹ 🙂
27															☹ 🙂
28															☹ 🙂
29															☹ 🙂
30															☹ 🙂
31															☹ 🙂

HEALTH & VITALS

Month _____

Year _____

Day	Heart Rate	Blood O2	Blood Pressure over	Blood Pressure	Weight	Temperature	Blood Glucose	Number of Falls	Inhaler Usage	Bruising?	Joint Pain?				Sleep Well
1															☹ ☺
2															☹ ☺
3															☹ ☺
4															☹ ☺
5															☹ ☺
6															☹ ☺
7															☹ ☺
8															☹ ☺
9															☹ ☺
10															☹ ☺
11															☹ ☺
12															☹ ☺
13															☹ ☺
14															☹ ☺
15															☹ ☺
16															☹ ☺
17															☹ ☺
18															☹ ☺
19															☹ ☺
20															☹ ☺
21															☹ ☺
22															☹ ☺
23															☹ ☺
24															☹ ☺
25															☹ ☺
26															☹ ☺
27															☹ ☺
28															☹ ☺
29															☹ ☺
30															☹ ☺
31															☹ ☺

HEALTH & VITALS

Month _____

Year _____

Day	Heart Rate	Blood O2	Blood Pressure over	Blood Pressure	Weight	Temperature	Blood Glucose	Number of Falls	Inhaler Usage	Bruising?	Joint Pain?			Sleep Well
1														☹ 🙂
2														☹ 🙂
3														☹ 🙂
4														☹ 🙂
5														☹ 🙂
6														☹ 🙂
7														☹ 🙂
8														☹ 🙂
9														☹ 🙂
10														☹ 🙂
11														☹ 🙂
12														☹ 🙂
13														☹ 🙂
14														☹ 🙂
15														☹ 🙂
16														☹ 🙂
17														☹ 🙂
18														☹ 🙂
19														☹ 🙂
20														☹ 🙂
21														☹ 🙂
22														☹ 🙂
23														☹ 🙂
24														☹ 🙂
25														☹ 🙂
26														☹ 🙂
27														☹ 🙂
28														☹ 🙂
29														☹ 🙂
30														☹ 🙂
31														☹ 🙂

HEALTH & VITALS

Month _____

Year _____

Day	Heart Rate	Blood O2	Blood Pressure over Blood Pressure	Weight	Temperature	Blood Glucose	Number of Falls	Inhaler Usage	Bruising?	Joint Pain?				Sleep Well
1														😐 😃
2														😐 😃
3														😐 😃
4														😐 😃
5														😐 😃
6														😐 😃
7														😐 😃
8														😐 😃
9														😐 😃
10														😐 😃
11														😐 😃
12														😐 😃
13														😐 😃
14														😐 😃
15														😐 😃
16														😐 😃
17														😐 😃
18														😐 😃
19														😐 😃
20														😐 😃
21														😐 😃
22														😐 😃
23														😐 😃
24														😐 😃
25														😐 😃
26														😐 😃
27														😐 😃
28														😐 😃
29														😐 😃
30														😐 😃
31														😐 😃

HEALTH & VITALS

Month _____

Year _____

Day	Heart Rate	Blood O2	Blood Pressure over	Blood Pressure	Weight	Temperature	Blood Glucose	Number of Falls	Inhaler Usage	Bruising?	Joint Pain?				Sleep Well
1															☹ ☺
2															☹ ☺
3															☹ ☺
4															☹ ☺
5															☹ ☺
6															☹ ☺
7															☹ ☺
8															☹ ☺
9															☹ ☺
10															☹ ☺
11															☹ ☺
12															☹ ☺
13															☹ ☺
14															☹ ☺
15															☹ ☺
16															☹ ☺
17															☹ ☺
18															☹ ☺
19															☹ ☺
20															☹ ☺
21															☹ ☺
22															☹ ☺
23															☹ ☺
24															☹ ☺
25															☹ ☺
26															☹ ☺
27															☹ ☺
28															☹ ☺
29															☹ ☺
30															☹ ☺
31															☹ ☺

HEALTH & VITALS

Month _____

Year _____

Day	Heart Rate	Blood O2	Blood Pressure over	Blood Pressure	Weight	Temperature	Blood Glucose	Number of Falls	Inhaler Usage	Bruising?	Joint Pain?			Sleep Well
1														😐 😊
2														😐 😊
3														😐 😊
4														😐 😊
5														😐 😊
6														😐 😊
7														😐 😊
8														😐 😊
9														😐 😊
10														😐 😊
11														😐 😊
12														😐 😊
13														😐 😊
14														😐 😊
15														😐 😊
16														😐 😊
17														😐 😊
18														😐 😊
19														😐 😊
20														😐 😊
21														😐 😊
22														😐 😊
23														😐 😊
24														😐 😊
25														😐 😊
26														😐 😊
27														😐 😊
28														😐 😊
29														😐 😊
30														😐 😊
31														😐 😊

HEALTH & VITALS

Month _____

Year _____

Day	Heart Rate	Blood O2	Blood Pressure over Blood Pressure	Weight	Temperature	Blood Glucose	Number of Falls	Inhaler Usage	Bruising?	Joint Pain?				Sleep Well
1														☹ 😊
2														☹ 😊
3														☹ 😊
4														☹ 😊
5														☹ 😊
6														☹ 😊
7														☹ 😊
8														☹ 😊
9														☹ 😊
10														☹ 😊
11														☹ 😊
12														☹ 😊
13														☹ 😊
14														☹ 😊
15														☹ 😊
16														☹ 😊
17														☹ 😊
18														☹ 😊
19														☹ 😊
20														☹ 😊
21														☹ 😊
22														☹ 😊
23														☹ 😊
24														☹ 😊
25														☹ 😊
26														☹ 😊
27														☹ 😊
28														☹ 😊
29														☹ 😊
30														☹ 😊
31														☹ 😊

HEALTH & VITALS

Month _____

Year _____

Day	Heart Rate	Blood O2	Blood Pressure over	Blood Pressure	Weight	Temperature	Blood Glucose	Number of Falls	Inhaler Usage	Bruising?	Joint Pain?				Sleep Well
1															☹ 😊
2															☹ 😊
3															☹ 😊
4															☹ 😊
5															☹ 😊
6															☹ 😊
7															☹ 😊
8															☹ 😊
9															☹ 😊
10															☹ 😊
11															☹ 😊
12															☹ 😊
13															☹ 😊
14															☹ 😊
15															☹ 😊
16															☹ 😊
17															☹ 😊
18															☹ 😊
19															☹ 😊
20															☹ 😊
21															☹ 😊
22															☹ 😊
23															☹ 😊
24															☹ 😊
25															☹ 😊
26															☹ 😊
27															☹ 😊
28															☹ 😊
29															☹ 😊
30															☹ 😊
31															☹ 😊

FRIENDS & FAMILY

NAME	_____
ADDRESS	_____
CITY _____ STATE _____ ZIP _____
PHONE _____ EMAIL _____

NAME	_____
ADDRESS	_____
CITY _____ STATE _____ ZIP _____
PHONE _____ EMAIL _____

NAME	_____
ADDRESS	_____
CITY _____ STATE _____ ZIP _____
PHONE _____ EMAIL _____

NAME	_____
ADDRESS	_____
CITY _____ STATE _____ ZIP _____
PHONE _____ EMAIL _____

NAME	_____
ADDRESS	_____
CITY _____ STATE _____ ZIP _____
PHONE _____ EMAIL _____

FRIENDS & FAMILY

NAME _____
ADDRESS _____
CITY _____ STATE _____ ZIP _____
PHONE _____ EMAIL _____

NAME _____
ADDRESS _____
CITY _____ STATE _____ ZIP _____
PHONE _____ EMAIL _____

NAME _____
ADDRESS _____
CITY _____ STATE _____ ZIP _____
PHONE _____ EMAIL _____

NAME _____
ADDRESS _____
CITY _____ STATE _____ ZIP _____
PHONE _____ EMAIL _____

NAME _____
ADDRESS _____
CITY _____ STATE _____ ZIP _____
PHONE _____ EMAIL _____

FRIENDS & FAMILY

NAME	_____
ADDRESS	_____
CITY _____	STATE _____ ZIP _____
PHONE _____	EMAIL _____

NAME	_____
ADDRESS	_____
CITY _____	STATE _____ ZIP _____
PHONE _____	EMAIL _____

NAME	_____
ADDRESS	_____
CITY _____	STATE _____ ZIP _____
PHONE _____	EMAIL _____

NAME	_____
ADDRESS	_____
CITY _____	STATE _____ ZIP _____
PHONE _____	EMAIL _____

NAME	_____
ADDRESS	_____
CITY _____	STATE _____ ZIP _____
PHONE _____	EMAIL _____

FRIENDS & FAMILY

NAME	
ADDRESS	
CITY _____ STATE _____ ZIP _____	
PHONE _____ EMAIL _____	

NAME	
ADDRESS	
CITY _____ STATE _____ ZIP _____	
PHONE _____ EMAIL _____	

NAME	
ADDRESS	
CITY _____ STATE _____ ZIP _____	
PHONE _____ EMAIL _____	

NAME	
ADDRESS	
CITY _____ STATE _____ ZIP _____	
PHONE _____ EMAIL _____	

NAME	
ADDRESS	
CITY _____ STATE _____ ZIP _____	
PHONE _____ EMAIL _____	

Made in the USA
Columbia, SC
06 June 2024